FOR THE SAKE OF THE CALL

A READY TO SING MISSIONS MINI-MUSICAL

Arranged by
RUSSELL MAULDIN

Created by
RUSSELL MAULDIN & SUE C. SMITH

AVAILABLE PRODUCTS:

Choral Book	45757-2824-7
CD Preview Pak	45757-2824-1
Listening CD	45757-2824-2
Split-Track Accompaniment CD	45757-2824-3
Audio Stem Files	45757-2824-4
Split-Track Accompaniment DVD	45757-2824-6
Orchestration/Conductor's Score CD-Rom	45757-2824-8
Soprano/Alto Rehearsal Track CD	45757-2824-0
Tenor/Bass Rehearsal Track CD	45757-2824-5

INSTRUMENTATION:
Rhythm • Drum Set • Flute 1, 2 • Oboe (Soprano Sax/Clarinet) • Clarinet 1, 2 • Trumpet 1 • Trumpet 2, 3 • Horn 1, 2 (Alto Sax 1, 2) • Trombone 1, 2 (Tenor Sax/Baritone T.C.) • Trombone 3 • Tuba (Bari Sax) • Percussion 1, 2 • Timpani Violin 1 • Violin 2 • Viola Cello • String Bass (Bass Clarinet/Bassoon) • String Reduction • Chord Chart

a division of

WWW.BRENTWOODBENSON.COM

© MMXV Brentwood-Benson Music Publications, 101 Winners Circle, Brentwood, TN 37027. All Rights Reserved. Unauthorized Duplication Prohibited.

Contents

For the Sake of the Call ---------------------------------------3

   with Send the Light

Win the Lost at Any Cost--------------------------------------20

   with Amazing Grace

Song for the Nations -------------------------------------29

   with For the Sake of the Call (Reprise)

For the Sake of the Call
with Send the Light

Words and Music by
STEVEN CURTIS CHAPMAN
Arranged by Russell Mauldin

NARRATOR: *(Music starts)* Standing on a hillside with His followers, Jesus gave them this great command just before He returned to His Father: "Go into all the world and preach the Gospel. Teach people to follow Me and do what I've said. I will always be with you!" *(Music change)* The mission was clear and those who devoted their lives to it changed the world forever.

© Copyright 1991 Universal Music - Brentwood Benson Songs / Sparrow Song / Greg Nelson Music (BMI)
(Administered at CapitolCMGPublishing.com). All rights reserved. Used by permission.
PLEASE NOTE: Copying of this music is NOT covered by the CCLI license. For CCLI information call 1-800-234-2446.

vot - ed to live and to die for the sake of the call.

No - bod - y stood and ap - plaud - ed them, so they

sake of the call. No oth-er rea-son at all but the sake of the call. Whol-ly de-vot-ed to live and to die for the sake of the

LADIES: call. Send the light to the world!

CHOIR: For the sake of the call!

Win the Lost at Any Cost

with Amazing Grace

Words and Music by
LEON H. ELLIS
Arranged by Russell Mauldin

NARRATOR: *(Music starts)* We know what Jesus has asked us to do, and yet sometimes we hesitate to follow. But the fields are white, and the harvest is ready. The need is great. Let us do whatever it takes to win souls to Christ.

© Copyright 1959 Church of God, Inc. (Administered by Music Services o/b/o Tennessee Music & Printing Company).
All rights reserved. Used by permission.
PLEASE NOTE: Copying of this music is NOT covered by the CCLI license. For CCLI information call 1-800-234-2446.

13
rip-ened un-to har-vest, yet so quick-ly comes the night.

Em7 | Am7 | C/D D7 | Gsus G

17 *LADIES*
Chris-tians must get bus-y; there is work to do.

MEN

C | Am | F A7/E | Dm

21 *ALL*
Here's an ur-gent task a-wait-ing you.

C/G | Fmaj7/G G7 | Csus | C Em/B

Song for the Nations
with For the Sake of the Call (Reprise)

Words and Music by
CHRIS CHRISTENSEN
Arranged by Russell Mauldin

NARRATOR: What will make the difference in whether people know Jesus or not? *(Music starts)* In whether they experience His love and mercy or miss the joy of a relationship with Him? In whether they are destined for eternity with Him or doomed to spend it separated from Him? It takes us sharing the simple story of who Jesus is and why He came. It requires us only to tell what He has done in our lives and what He wants to do for every man, woman, boy and girl. Who will answer the call today?

© Copyright 1986 Integrity's Hosanna! Music (ASCAP) (Administered at CapitolCMGPublishing.com). All rights reserved. Used by permission.
PLEASE NOTE: Copying of this music is NOT covered by the CCLI license. For CCLI information call 1-800-234-2446.

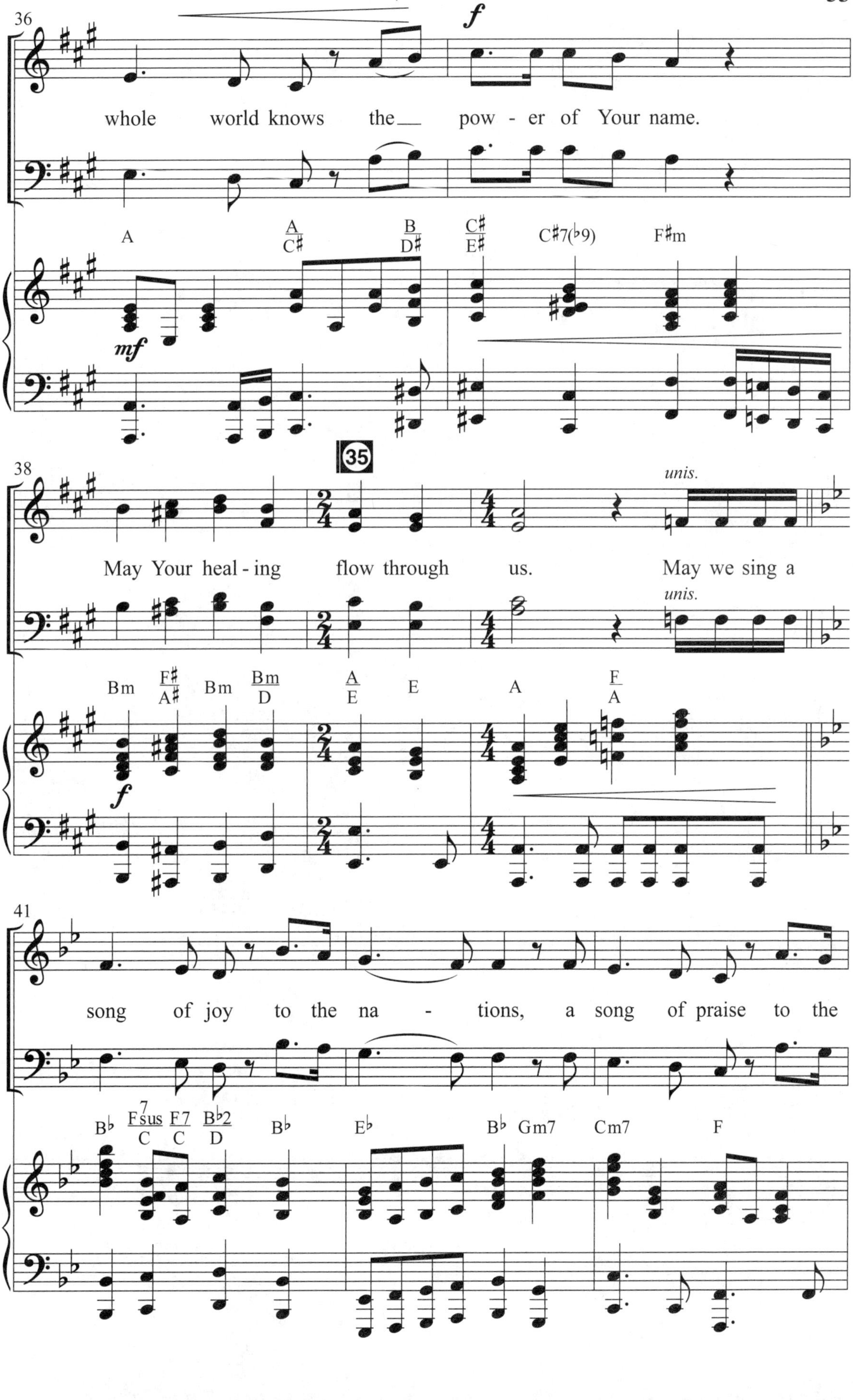
36
f
whole world knows the pow - er of Your name.
A
A/C♯
B/D♯
C♯/E♯
C♯7(♭9)
F♯m
mf
38
35
unis.
May Your heal - ing flow through us. May we sing a
Bm
F♯/A♯
Bm
Bm/D
A/E
E
A
F/A
f
41
song of joy to the na - tions, a song of praise to the
B♭
F7sus/C
F7/C
B♭2/D
B♭
E♭
B♭
Gm7
Cm7
F

May Your kingdom come to the nations, Your will be done in the peoples of the earth, till the whole world knows that Jesus Christ is Lord.

FOR THE SAKE OF THE CALL (Steven Curtis Chapman)

We will abandon it all for the sake of the call. No other reason at all but the sake of the call.

© Copyright 1991 Universal Music - Brentwood Benson Songs / Sparrow Song / Greg Nelson Music (BMI)
(Administered at CapitolCMGPublishing.com). All rights reserved. Used by permission.

11 Best-Selling EASTER MUSICALS
from the READY TO SING SERIES
America's #1 Selling Church Choir Series
Arranged by RUSSELL MAULDIN

These musicals are perfect for the small to medium-sized choir, or the large choir with limited rehearsal time. Available in Easy SATB.

ORDER YOUR PREVIEW PAK
TODAY!

The Ready To Sing Series available - Exclusively through the **Brentwood Choral Club!**

Call **1-800-846-7664**, visit **www.brentwoodbenson.com** or **order from your local Christian retailer today!**